NO LONGER PROPERTY OF
SEATTLE PUBLIC LIBRARY

D0359739

NO LONGER PROPERTY OF
SEATTLE PUBLIC LIBRARY

A LITTLE BIT

OF

SHAMANISM

A LITTLE BIT
OF
SHAMANISM

AN INTRODUCTION TO
SHAMANIC JOURNEYING

ANA CAMPOS

STERLING ETHOS

New York

DEDICATION

To the ancestors and the descendants, for the hope of healing our home

To all who want to gather with open hearts and open minds

To Nathaniel, Gwyndha, Bran, Oona, and Heulwenn

STERLING ETHOS
New York

An Imprint of Sterling Publishing
1166 Avenue of the Americas
New York, NY 10036

STERLING ETHOS and the distinctive Sterling Ethos logo are
registered trademarks of Sterling Publishing Co., Inc.

© 2019 Ana Campos
Cover © 2019 Sterling Publishing Co., Inc.

All rights reserved. No part of this publication may be reproduced, stored in a retrieval system, or
transmitted in any form or by any means (including electronic, mechanical, photocopying, recording,
or otherwise) without prior written permission from the publisher.

ISBN 978-1-4549-3375-5

Distributed in Canada by Sterling Publishing Co., Inc.
c/o Canadian Manda Group, 664 Annette Street
Toronto, Ontario M6S 2C8, Canada
Distributed in the United Kingdom by GMC Distribution Services
Castle Place, 166 High Street, Lewes, East Sussex BN7 1XU, England
Distributed in Australia by NewSouth Books
University of New South *Wales, Sydney, NSW 2052, Australia*

For information about custom editions, special sales, and premium and corporate purchases, please
contact Sterling Special Sales at 800-805-5489 or specialsales@sterlingpublishing.com.

Manufactured in Canada

2 4 6 8 10 9 7 5 3 1

sterlingpublishing.com

Interior design by Gina Bonanno
Cover design by Elizabeth Mihaltse Lindy

Image Credits: Shutterstock (cover, throughout): 1008; satit_srihin

CONTENTS

INTRODUCTION

Tell them that we want our voices to be heard.
The earth needs healing before it is too late.

A small group of people are gathered in a darkened room, lying on their backs with their eyes closed. The smell of sage smoke lingers in the air, and rhythmic drumming fills the space. I am watching over the group as I drum them into non-ordinary reality to meet with their helping spirits. I often stay in ordinary reality when drumming for others, but today I can feel my spirit guides tugging at the edges of my consciousness. I close my eyes and tumble into the spirit realm faster than I ever have. My helping spirits know I am writing a book, and they have something to say.

Tell them that we want our voices to be heard. The earth needs healing before it is too late.

This is the message my helping spirits asked me to share. Our helping spirits have been calling to us for a long time, and more of us are finally starting to listen. If you are reading this book, it might be out of simple curiosity. If that is the case, read on with an open mind; you might be surprised to see a new path open before you. It is more likely than not, though, that you are in the midst of an important shift in your life. Something has been calling to you, and you are searching for answers. Perhaps you are looking to feel more connected to the earth, or you are searching for answers and a connection to something bigger. You may have experienced trauma and are seeking a path toward healing. No matter what drew you here, Shamanism has the ability to bring profound transformation into your life if you make room for it.

The defining characteristic of Shamanism is an active, voluntary relationship with our guides and helping spirits, cultivated through access to non-ordinary reality. This is something we can all benefit from. Shamanism provides us with a framework and methodology to start developing and cultivating these relationships. Our helping spirits are present in our lives, whether or not we are aware of them or acknowledge them. But if we start collaborating with them, we are opening ourselves up to growth. With collaboration, these relationships can bring us new levels of wisdom and help us heal ourselves. A regular shamanic practice can bring true inner transformation to those who open themselves up to it, which in turn, can have countless positive effects in our lives.

In this book, I will provide a basic but comprehensive guide to Shamanism for anyone looking to start their own personal shamanic practice to enhance their lives and heal themselves. You will learn how to use alpha states and shamanic journeying to establish a healthy working relationship with your helping spirits, who can become a lifelong support system for you. While this book will provide you with a solid foundation, there is always more to be learned about Shamanism. I strongly encourage those who feel the call to walk this path to continue studying, through personal research and with mentors if the opportunity presents itself. But most importantly, always remember that Shamanism is something you live and experience, and your spirit guides will always be your best teachers.

What this book will not do is make you a shaman or healer. While all of us can develop a shamanic practice to enhance our own lives, becoming a shaman is something we do not get to decide for ourselves. A shaman or shamanic healer is not just someone who uses shamanic practices in their personal lives, but someone who lives in service of their community. Our helping spirits may decide that is the right path for us, or we may become recognized as healers within our community based on the work we do. That is a call that may or may not come to you as you continue on your path, but either way, you can still benefit greatly from a personal shamanic practice. Not everyone wants to become a shaman or healer, but all of us want to create shifts in our lives so we can break the patterns and cycles that have caused and continue to cause suffering. Bringing healing into your own life should be your first and foremost goal as you embark on this journey.

In this book, I am sharing with you knowledge I have gathered over years of study and practice in different continents and with various teachers. My goal is not to present you with an absolute truth, which would be beyond my capabilities, but rather with a collection of experiences that can serve as a stepping stone for your own path.

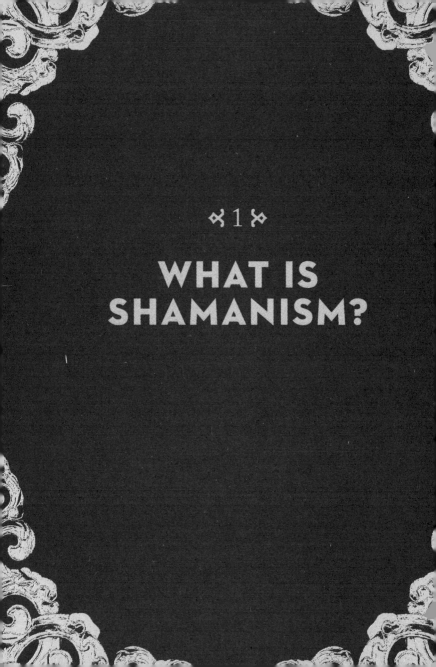

❖ 1 ❖

WHAT IS SHAMANISM?

THE ORIGIN OF THE WORD *SHAMANISM* IS A BIT COMplicated, and at times, a bit fraught. Throughout the history of humankind, every tribe has had their healer or healers, and each culture has their own term for these healers. They have been known as *curanderos, pajés, strega, mães de santo,* and countless other names. The term *shaman* originated from an indigenous tribe in Siberia but was not used globally until modern times. *Shaman* was the term for healer within this specific Siberian tribe and their culture. In recent history, however, the term *shamanism* has been used by Western anthropologists to describe a collection of ceremonial techniques seen in the ritual practices of several indigenous tribes across the globe, and highlights the common elements seen across many of these cultures. It shows us that similar techniques were discovered by medicine people all over the world, people who did not have contact with one another and nonetheless arrived at strikingly similar practices. The value in recognizing these near-universal elements is in realizing that spirit has been calling to all of us in similar ways, throughout the history of humankind. As different medicine people dedicated themselves to connecting with non-ordinary reality and uncovering how our helping spirits want to communicate with us, they came back with surprisingly similar answers. These methodologies are part of all our heritages, and this ancestral knowledge is encoded in our DNA.

The popularity of the words *shaman* and *shamanism* is due in great part to the work of the late Michael Harner, an anthropologist who became a shamanic practitioner through years of visiting and studying with various indigenous tribes across the world. As he observed common elements from culture to culture, the concept of universal (or semi-universal) shamanic practices emerged, giving form to Modern Shamanism. More specifically, he observed the use of altered states to enter non-ordinary reality and forge an intentional working relationship with helping spirits. Harner himself referred to this as Core Shamanism. But it is extremely important to understand that most indigenous practitioners do not call themselves shamans, instead using the terms specific to their own culture. In this book, we will not be exploring the practices or rites of a specific culture, but rather, a system of techniques any of us can use to bring healing into our lives. For the sake of simplicity, I will be using the terms *shamanism* and *shamanic practice*, but I urge readers to understand this is a simplification and that the study of these practices warrants an understanding of cultural context.

As we have discussed, Shamanism refers to a system of common elements seen across many cultures. This means Shamanism is not a religion, and it is non-dogmatic and uncodified. Shamanism will not tell you which deity to worship because Shamanism is not exclusive to a single cosmology. It is actually quite the opposite, since shamanic practices are found within various cosmologies around the world, which supports the idea of a source that is older and more expansive than modern concepts of divinity. Shamanism is experiential, and completely personal. This practice is a system of direct revelation, meaning that it is not ritual performed by others and watched by spectators, but an experience every practitioner engages in. All shamanic practitioners engage in ritual and ceremony as they develop a working, intimate relationship with their helping spirits. The techniques of Shamanism connect us to Spirit or the Source, in whatever way you define it. These methodologies center on rituals that engage one or more of the physical senses as a way to trigger alpha states and allow the practitioner to go on shamanic journeys. The use of these trance states is central to shamanic practice, and something that we are all capable of. It is important to note that entering trance or altered states is something that is an innate part of every person and can be achieved through many different methods. Within the shamanic framework, altered states are used for the specific purpose of connecting with helping spirits.

Shamanic practices can take many different forms across cultures. As an example, Reiki is a Japanese healing system based on the deliberate and directed use of *ki*, a Japanese term for vital energy. Reiki has been described as Japanese Shamanism, a concept studied and expanded by Jim PathFinder Ewing. Ewing discusses the method through which Reiki was devised as shamanic in nature. Dr. Mikao Usui, the creator of Reiki, received the Reiki symbols during a period of reclusion, a common initiatory process in some indigenous practices. Grace Walsh, a direct student of Ewing's and one of my teachers, explains the term *shaman* as, "one who sees in the dark." Reiki allows us to engage in healing, of ourselves and others, beyond physical ailments, reaching both the emotional and spiritual levels. When healing with Reiki, we are stepping outside of ordinary reality to see beyond physical trauma, seeing what lies "in the dark." Reiki also embodies the concept of hollow bone, discussed later in this book, where practitioners act as conduits for ki.

In my native Brazil, we have indigenous groups who still practice their ancestral ceremonies and live according to their ancient traditions. They have developed their own contextual practices, such as using plant and animal poisons found in their environment for healing rites and the expansion of consciousness. In the Tupi-Guarani cultures, the medicine folks are *pajés*. We also have Candomblé, a cultural spiritual system that was born out of the African practices brought over by slaves and evolved within the context of the land and spirits of Brazil. What all these different cultural systems and practices have in common is that they emphasize a connection to what exists beyond ordinary reality, accessing this connection, and doing so from a first-person, direct revelation perspective.

WHAT OR WHO ARE SHAMANS?

EVERY PERSON WHO INTEGRATES SHAMANIC practices and/or ceremonies into their lives is a shamanic practitioner to some degree. Shamans are shamanic practitioners who have dedicated their spiritual practice to helping others in their community.

Not every shamanic practitioner is a shaman, in the same way that not everyone who works on healing themselves is a healer (and not everyone who receives medical treatment becomes a medical doctor). The distinction between a shamanic practitioner and a shaman is an important one. Everyone on this path must first heal themselves, and only then can they start to consider being in service to their community. Folks who come to study shamanic work to heal themselves and their environment are shamanic practitioners.

It is also important to distinguish between shamans and clergy. In some cultures, the two overlap, but this is not always the case. Members of the clergy lead the community in devotional practices usually within established frameworks that have been passed down in a traditional manner. While these rituals do provide a means for honoring spirit, their intent is not to bring participants into non-ordinary reality to directly communicate with helping spirits. A community can have shamans who also function as clergy, but in some communities they have distinct roles, with the shaman tending to the working relationships with helping spirits and the clergy tending to ritual and liturgy. As discussed in the previous chapter, shamanism is non-dogmatic and is not a cosmology unto itself. Clergy, on the other hand, function within their specific dogmas and cosmologies.

This means that becoming a shaman is not akin to becoming a priest or priestess, but it is still a path that requires extensive devotion and commitment. Once a practitioner transitions into performing ceremony and healing for other people, they are on their way to becoming shamans. A teacher once described shamans as the original activists, because they are the ones seeking to bring harmony and balance among people, the earth, and the realm of spirit. Before engaging in that work, we must first bring harmony to ourselves. A shaman has, after years of practice, chosen a position of service to their community and their land. They are there to help bring healing and harmony and help others with their shamanic practice. Not every shamanic practitioner will become a shaman, and that's perfectly fine. Each of us has a path to follow, and not all of us will be called onto a path of service. As you embark on this journey, do so without preconceptions or expectations, and let your helping spirits guide you on your path, whether it be as a practitioner or whether you hear a calling to teach and guide others.

Shamanic practitioners can come from any background, be from any culture, and be of any gender. While I have witnessed gender discrimination against female practitioners within modern shamanic practices, there is no historical basis for this. In *The Norse Shaman*, Evelyn Rysdyk discusses gender in Shamanism, presenting archeological evidence of prehistoric female shamans, such as the shaman at Dolni Věstonice in the Czech Republic, and the shaman uncovered in what is now northern Israel.

The key defining element of a shamanic practitioner is their personal commitment to study, practice, and grow and to develop an intimate working relationship with their helping spirits. The working relationship is developed through a regular practice of accessing nonordinary reality, which will be discussed later in this book.

❧ 3 ❧

LINEAGE, HERITAGE, AND CULTURAL APPROPRIATION

IN A PREVIOUS SECTION OF THIS BOOK, WE TOUCHED on the complicated history of the term *shamanism*. Anyone who seeks a deeper connection to Spirit can study Shamanism and use these elements in their personal practice. But as humans existing in a world where privilege, oppression, colonialism, and cultural appropriation still exist, we need to keep these topics at the forefront of any discussion about Shamanism. I urge anyone bringing Shamanism into their personal practice to do so from a place of respect and humility, with an understanding of how their own personal heritage intersects with the knowledge they are acquiring.

A big question that is important to address is: can non-indigenous people practice Shamanism? The short answer is yes, but they must do so with proper respect. Shamanism is not something that should be approached as a fad, fashion statement, or business plan.

11

To be a shamanic practitioner is to focus on an internal process of transformation. It is to develop a genuine, ongoing working relationship with our helping spirits, and to properly honor the shamanic practitioners who came before us, and who are still here today. I have come across teachers and practitioners who handle this question by saying that Shamanism is everyone's birthright. While this is not necessarily inaccurate, the reality is that the answer to this question is, and should be, much more complicated.

While Shamanism is a methodology, not a religion, and does not belong to one religious group, culture, race, or country, it has undeniably been brought to us by indigenous groups. In acknowledging this, we must recognize that many, if not all, indigenous groups these teachings came from have faced discrimination or oppression in some form. Even in present times, this oppression continues, as sacred native lands are defaced and exploited in the name of capitalism. As students, we have a duty to approach the study of Shamanism with the appropriate level of respect it deserves. We must understand where these practices come from and honor the people who brought us these teachings.

Lewis Mehl-Madrona, whose research has focused on the Cherokee and Lakota traditions, has spoken of cultural appropriation and the respectful practice of Shamanism. He explains that the indigenous communities of North America are upset at those who play at being indigenous. He uses the example of those who attend one or two workshops and then take it upon themselves to start teaching and leading ceremonies. As we discussed earlier in this book, developing a shamanic practice does not automatically make one a shaman or healer. This kind of behavior trivializes the dedicated study and practice, generally spanning several years, that is expected within shamanic traditions. On the other hand, sincere seekers and students of all backgrounds are generally welcomed. We all have the ability to forge strong connections with helping spirits, and our intent is what matters the most.

I had the great pleasure of speaking to Alonso del Rio, a Peruvian *curandero* (healer), regarding the contemporary practice of Shamanism. Alonso spent over a decade as an apprentice in the Peruvian Amazon jungle, learning about the *plantas maestras* (master plants) from the Shipibo tribe. I asked him to share his thoughts on how non-indigenous people can develop an appropriate and respectful shamanic practice. His main message centered around respect, first and foremost, which resonates with the message shared by Lewis Mehl-Madrona. We must have respect for the origins of the ceremonies we are using and understand these origins. If we use ceremonies outside of their cultural context, they lose meaning. The goal of shamanic practice is the expansion of consciousness, and respect is the necessary first step.

Alonso used the example of tourists visiting indigenous tribes in the Amazon and witnessing traditional ceremonies. It is not uncommon for visitors to record these ceremonies, taking them back to their own homes and mimicking them. In this sort of practice, we see a fundamental misunderstanding of the origin of ceremony. When a medicine person develops a sacred song or a ceremony, this is something that came out of close, deep ritual work with both their helping spirits and the spirits of their land. If one were to witness one of these rites and simply memorize it to use upon return to their own home, the meaning and connection of the rite would be completely lost. Not only is this behavior disrespectful, but it is also ineffective because the ceremony has been stripped of the elements that give it power.

Alonso also discussed the use of the word *shamanism*, reminding us that this generalized terminology was brought to us by Western academics. If we return to the origin of the word *shaman*, it would be accurate to say there are no shamans on the American continents, as this word was never part of the vocabulary of any American indigenous communities. Perhaps we should consider a rejection of this word entirely, since it was used by a specific Siberian group and did not apply to the healers of the Americas, Europe, or Oceania. Alonso encourages us to remember that our ceremonial practices need to exist within the context of our lives and our own communities. We all have a connection to the land we were born in and the land we live on. Rather than focusing our energy on learning and co-opting the rites and traditions of other people, we can benefit the most by engaging within our own cultural context. As we develop our relationships with our own helping spirits, they will teach us the rites, songs, and ceremonies that belong to us.

I also had a wonderful conversation with my friend Liza Fenster, also known as Crow Mother, about respectful practice while preparing for this book. She teaches Reiki and Shamanism and has a healing practice in Brooklyn, New York. Liza was raised by a single mother from Puerto Rico, and throughout her childhood, her family intertwined their Taino heritage and traditions into their everyday lives. Today she still leans toward traditional Caribbean indigenous practices, honoring her Taino roots, but continues to study with a variety of teachers. As an adult, Liza found her father and discovered she has Hopi and Cherokee ancestry. As we talked about how to approach shamanic practice within a Western context—between her mixed indigenous background and mine as an immigrant—we were able to distill our conversation into one key question: Are you a steward of the earth?

This is the question we should always hold at our core, and it is a concept worth unpacking further. In my conversation with Alonso, he said something that really stuck with me: "Heal yourself first, and then let's see about everything else." We were having a discussion about an upsetting trend of people coming to healing and shamanic work not with the goal of healing themselves, but with the goal of pursuing this as a business practice. Liza and I also discussed this, and voiced our disappointment in a growing trend of shamanic workshops being offered from a business perspective, promising viable self-employment as the end goal. This is unfortunate, to say the least, because practitioners are losing sight of the purpose of their practice. Shamanic ceremonies existed long before the capitalist business model, and they were necessary to ensure the survival of the group. As I mentioned earlier, a teacher once said that shamans were the original activists, since their goal was to promote harmony among the individual, the community, and the environment. Part of the shaman's responsibility was, historically, to communicate with the spirit realm to glean information on the movements of herds, which would provide food for the community. Today we live in a much different socioeconomic context, and our physical survival no longer depends on such a deep connection with the spirits of the land. This has created room for a misinterpretation of the goals of shamanic work, and so we see those who have lost their focus, prioritizing financial gain over spiritual healing.

This brings us back to the question of how non-indigenous folks can practice Shamanism from a place of respect. Liza summarized this as, anyone is welcome in these healing practices if their intent is coming from a genuine place. If your goal is to heal the earth and all of her people, then you are approaching this work from a place of respect, which is more important than your place of origin. But while this is a great place to start, it is also important to take this one step farther. Our indigenous communities are hurting. It is undeniably wrong for non-indigenous people to be profiting financially from shamanic work while indigenous people are struggling. So as you embark on your journey, always remember to ask yourself what you can do to support indigenous people. You cannot be in harmony with the earth if you are not advocating for all her people.

It starts with a respectful practice and the basic notion of not taking credit for ideas that aren't ours. As practitioners with genuine intent, we should not claim the specific ritual rites, tools, or ceremonial dress of any culture or tribe we have not personally learned from. It is one thing to be handed down a ceremony from a teacher, and another to witness and copy. For example, rattles are used in many shamanic practices around the world. This is a common ritual tool, and I do encourage those interested in developing a shamanic practice to invest in one. However, I would advise against purchasing a rattle covered in symbols that are specific to a tribe or culture that you are unfamiliar with. Find the ritual rattle that is right for you and makes sense within the context of your practice. By extension, do not purchase or mimic the ritual garb of practices that aren't yours; don't adopt ceremonial jewelry without understanding its significance, and so forth. Be true and honest about where you came from and where you are going.

Discernment is as important as respect in the development of a spiritual practice. If you are interested in truly approaching your practice in a way that is in harmony with your surroundings, consider approaching the acquisition of your tools the way our ancestors did: by crafting them yourself. Alonso del Rio spoke of this issue, using the example of feathers and feather fans that are commonly used in ceremony. These tools used to be fashioned from birds who had died naturally, their feathers harvested with respect and ceremony to be crafted into ritual items. Nowadays, many people are buying their tools online or from trendy boutiques, with no knowledge of which birds their feathers are coming from and no information on how they died and how their parts were harvested. Similarly, we can order animal-hide drums without having any knowledge of their origin. While it might not be feasible for everyone to return to crafting their own ritual tools, we do have a responsibility to understand where they are coming from. We can choose to source them from people who are crafting tools with the proper respect, as opposed to mass-produced sources where the ceremony is entirely lost. We can engage in gathering and find feathers naturally left behind by the birds that live on our land.

All this said, there is always more that can be done. Not taking credit for work that isn't yours and treating the tools and customs of indigenous folks with proper respect is a first step, but I encourage each of us to go farther. Supporting indigenous communities goes beyond avoiding active disrespect. We can instead become active participants in supporting and advocating for communities in need. If you are benefiting from indigenous knowledge and ceremonies, be sure to find ways you can circle back and support these communities. As part of your studies, develop an understanding of sacred native lands, and do your part to protect them. Get involved in efforts that support their needs, but do this with one caveat—never approach this outreach with the assumption that indigenous communities need to be taught different ways to live. To do so in this manner is to approach the communities that are benefitting you from a place of ego, with an assumption that your culture knows better. Always check in with your genuine intent and humility as you travel along your path. Be willing to listen and be an ally from a place of understanding.

I have had many conversations with another good friend who is an American shamanic practitioner of European descent. She has discussed her discomfort with workshops where the rites of a specific indigenous culture are taught without the appropriate cultural context.

I have noted previously that a lack of context for ceremony is disrespectful and harmful, and that as teachers and students, we should strive to do better. In her studies, she has chosen to practice respect by focusing her education on looking at near-universal ritual practices rather than pursuing a Native American tradition. Beyond this, she has been studying in a Druidry program to reconnect with her own ancient Celtic roots. As she explains it, she is striving to understand what it means to be a modern, European-descended female shamanic practitioner in the twenty-first-century United States. We must all practice Shamanism within the context of ourselves and our lives and understand how we fit into the larger picture of our communities.

As you further your studies and connect with shamanic teachers, understand their lineage and heritage. I define the distinction between lineage and heritage as the people we have learned from, as opposed to those who are our blood ancestors. Be ready to ask questions and develop an understanding of where you will fit into this lineage. Before you embark on an ongoing apprenticeship with a teacher, do your due diligence in understanding if they are coming to this work from a place of genuine intent. For the sake of transparency, I will share my lineage. I was born in Brazil, where I spent most of my formative years before moving to North America. I also spent part of my childhood in Europe and Asia. My ceremonial studies started in Brazil in the 1990s. In 2000, I joined a group and became an apprentice under a matriarch leading a ritual practice rooted in shamanic ceremonies. This matriarch is my oldest teacher, and I continue to work with and learn from her to this day, despite our living on different continents. She encourages me to study as much as possible and learn from many different teachers, which I continue to actively pursue.

For the sake of transparency, I will share my lineage. I was born in Brazil, where I spent most of my formative years before moving to North America. I also spent part of my childhood in Europe and Asia. My ceremonial studies started in Brazil in the 1990s. In 2000, I joined a group and became an apprentice under Gwyndha, a High Priestess and matriarch leading a ritual practice rooted in shamanic ceremonies. Gwyndha is my oldest teacher, and I continue to work with and learn from her to this day, despite our living on different continents. She encourages me to study as much as possible and learn from many different teachers, which I continue to actively pursue.

Since moving to the United States, I have studied with various shamanic teachers, through individual workshops and more prolonged apprenticeships. My teachers have come from a variety of backgrounds, including indigenous ancestry within the North American continent. Under Grace Walsh, I have studied ceremony and Reiki Shamanism, exploring the intersection of different cultural approaches to non-ordinary reality. I have also taken workshops through the Foundation for Shamanic Studies, which is the work of the late Michael Harner, whom I discussed earlier in this book. While this is not an exhaustive list of every teacher I have studied with, both within Shamanism and other metaphysical disciplines, I am honored by and grateful to all the teachers who have been willing to share their wisdom with me.

One final caveat: Everything presented in this book reflects my personal experience and learning. It is important to remember that Shamanism is not a spectator practice, and if you pursue this path, you will develop your own relationship with Spirit and your guides, as well as your own understanding of ceremonial work. It will overlap with my experiences in some instances and differ in others. There is no correct or prescribed shamanic experience or practice, and therefore, there is no incorrect shamanic experience. The key to your practice is to be in a working relationship with your helping spirits and to approach your practice from a place of authenticity. Always keep this in mind and remember that discernment and respect are your most important tools.

THE THREE
WORLDS MODEL

THE THREE WORLDS MODEL IS A COMMON BELIEF across shamanic practices and defines how reality is set up, with reality divided into Lower World, Middle World, and Upper World. Many journey practices are built around this belief; but while it is common, it is not universal. Several cultures travel to both Lower World and Upper World, but some travel to only one or the other. As you gain experience with journeying, I encourage you to visit the realms that call to you and decide for yourself what best fits into your practice.

While the Three Worlds Model is common, it is very important to understand that it is not a cosmology. The original indigenous cultures did have cosmologies that accompanied their shamanic ceremonies, but Core Shamanism as it is disseminated today does not. This is not necessarily a criticism, as there are benefits to a methodology that any of us can apply to our own cosmologies, but it is fundamental for your own practice to understand this distinction. Christina Pratt, director of the Last Mask Center for Shamanic Healing, explains cosmology as the science of the origin and development of the universe. Cosmologies are the stories that tell us where we came from, how life as we understand it began, and of the beings and places that exist here. These stories also explain the relationships between these beings and places, and provide us with a framework for understanding the world. Everyone has a cosmology, whether or not they are aware of this, and we subconsciously use our cosmologies as a lens to understand the world. Cosmologies can be scientific, religious, or somewhere in between. As we begin to analyze our own cosmologies, we can start to be more intentional in our stories, rather than moving through the world with preconceptions we have accepted by default from our upbringing.

In the shamanic Three Worlds Model, there are three main planes of existence, two of which can be accessed only by entering non-ordinary reality. These realms were not invented by shamanic practitioners, but rather discovered by them through journeys to non-ordinary reality. This is a commonality found in most shamanic practices, and many non-shamanic traditions. However, the Three Worlds Model does not contain the stories of the whys and the hows. Instead, this model defines what already is. How one experiences these realms, and how the spirits present themselves within these realms, is where one's personal cosmology factors in. Rather than a cosmology, the Three Worlds Model is an explanation of commonalities across shamanic cultures.

The mythology of the World Tree can function as a metaphor for the Three Worlds Model. This mythological archetype exists in the stories of many cultures, such as Norse, Mesoamerican, and Siberian. The World Tree is all-encompassing, with deep roots that ground it in the earth, a body that flowers and bears fruit, and the tallest of the branches reaching far into the sky. The roots correspond to Lower World, the trunk of the tree represents Middle World, and the tallest branches reflect Upper World. The physical realm we inhabit along with all incarnate beings is referred to as Middle World, which is perceived in ordinary reality. Lower and Upper Worlds exist in nonordinary reality and can be accessed with our non-physical bodies through journeying. Middle World also has a spiritual dimension we can journey to.

In non-ordinary reality, we encounter a variety of spirit forms. The spirits found in Lower and Upper Worlds are generally referred to as compassionate spirits, meaning they are benevolent forces and willing to provide help to those of us in the incarnate plane. However, not all spirits are compassionate. Non-ordinary reality is complex, much like ordinary reality, and in addition to compassionate spirits, we can also encounter neutral or harmful spirits. They can be the spirits of people who passed away but did not successfully cross over, or perhaps elemental spirits. I do not recommend journeying in Middle World until you have experience in journeying to both

Lower and Upper Worlds and have established an intimate working relationship with your helping spirits. Once you have this relationship, you can call upon your helping spirits to guide and protect you for a journey in Middle World. There are definitely valuable lessons to be learned in the spiritual dimension of our incarnate realm. In Shamanism, there is the basic belief that everything has its own energetic field or spirit. By journeying in Middle World, you can communicate and establish a relationship with the plants, animals, land, and elements around you. Through this experience, you can learn how to better live in harmony with your surroundings.

Lower World is below Middle World. Some shamanic paths refer to Lower World as Underworld, and while that terminology does not resonate with me, you might prefer it. Lower World is where we can connect with the essences and archetypes of nature, and our own primal selves. It is the home of animal spirits and plant spirits, our helping spirits that exist in non-human form. Visiting Lower World helps us remember and understand our place in nature, and it reminds us of the interconnectedness of all organisms. Lower World is accessed through a passageway that leads us into the depths of the earth. At the end of this passageway, we pass through a portal that takes us into a new landscape. This landscape is usually earthy and rich, deeply grounded. Lower World can look very similar to Middle World or take on otherworldly qualities. It is not uncommon to find unusual colors or odd proportions, and the laws of physics do not necessarily apply in the same way as they do in Middle World.

We may find ourselves much larger or smaller than usual, and it is common to experience giant plant or animal life.

Upper World is above Middle World and is usually the home of human-form helping spirits. Upper World is accessed by traveling upward into the skies until we cross a threshold. This threshold is critical, because if we do not cross this threshold, we can keep traveling upward in Middle World endlessly. Upper World has, in my experience, a much lighter and more airy feel than Lower World. The colors tend to be lighter, softer, and more pastel. Sometimes we find structures and temples in Upper World. While Lower World tends to be a more grounded and visceral experience, Upper World tends to be more intellectual. Where Lower World helps us remember our place in nature and connects us with our primal selves, Upper World helps us push the limits of our intellect and understanding. While we generally find animal spirits in Lower World, and human-form helping spirits in Upper World, spirits can move freely between realms, so you may encounter them in any of the three realms.

❖ 5 ❖

DEVELOPING A SHAMANIC PRACTICE

ALTHOUGH JOURNEYING TO MEET WITH OUR helping spirits is a keystone of shamanic practice, it is certainly not the only component. The journeys themselves are extremely important, but equally important is the integration process. Integration refers to the way in which we bring the lessons of Shamanism into our daily lives. This process involves both acting upon the knowledge we receive from our helping spirits and moving through our lives in a more intentional way.

We have to make a conscious decision to allow the sacred to permeate our lives. A young man approached me after a shamanic workshop to ask for advice. He told me that he was regularly immersing himself in ceremony but still finding himself disconnected from nature and spirit in his daily life. He had dedicated ceremony days where he would cleanse his space, set up his altar, honor the directions, and then spend time in sacred space connecting with spirits and working on healing. But outside of these dedicated ceremony days, he was feeling disconnected from his spiritual work. As we talked further, he explained that he kept a rather strict separation between his spiritual work and his mundane life, due to the nature of his profession. My suggestion was to reframe the way he saw the split between the sacred and the mundane and to find ways to see the sacred in the everyday, both inside and outside of ceremony. If we can understand that we carry the sacred with us always, we can realize our connection to spirit is constant, even when we are not engaging in elaborate rituals. Ceremony is more than just specific rituals, and if you allow it to, it can become a way of life. As we begin to see the sacred in the everyday, we can begin to realize that all aspects of life are also sacred.

Even the simplest, most mundane act can be sacred if performed with the right intent. This young man had two issues stemming from his situation: maintaining privacy and performing integration. In reality, these two concepts do not have to be at odds. Integration is the process of bringing the lessons of our spiritual work into our mundane lives. This is a constant, ongoing process that we will continually undertake throughout our lives, because it is never complete. However, it is essential because spiritual and emotional shifts do not result in a changed life if we do not bring those lessons into the mundane realm. When we are able to see the sacred in all aspects of our lives, we will find ourselves moving through the world with more care, gratitude, and intent. This is the beginning and basis of creating a shamanic practice.

There are many behaviors we engage in without realizing how meaningful they really are. The most obvious example of this is in the way we use our voices. Our voices are our most basic ceremonial tool, holding the power to shape our lives. At the very least, we should be mindful of our words so that we are not putting energies into motion that we do not intend to. The power of words is such a widespread metaphysical concept that it is seen in practices across the world. For example, in Kabbalah, a form of Jewish mysticism, language holds the power of creation. Reality is created through words. Whenever we write or speak, we are in relationship with the element of air. Our helping spirits pay attention to what we say, so it behooves us to use discernment and be intentional.

Another behavior I would like to discuss is the smoking of tobacco, because it is such a common Western habit. Mainstream tobacco smoking has long been disconnected from its ancient ceremonial origins. Commercial cigarettes, with all their additives, are a far cry from the pure tobacco leaves smoked by indigenous groups in a ritual setting. However, tobacco is still present in the mainstream and it is being used casually. In many Native American and indigenous Mesoamerican cultures, tobacco is considered sacred. More specifically, it is believed that when one smokes tobacco, the spirits come to listen to our thoughts and words, considering them prayers. If we are not intentional in how we are engaging in that behavior, we may find our unintentional or unwanted prayers answered. For those who choose to smoke cigarettes, I suggest becoming aware of the thoughts and words you are projecting while engaging in that behavior. I often think of the people I see standing outside on work breaks, complaining about their lives as they smoke. Are those really the messages anyone wants to be sending to spirit? For those of us who do not smoke, if we choose to incorporate tobacco into our ceremonies, we can do this by burning pure tobacco leaves in a fire-safe dish. As you burn these herbs, choose your words carefully and ask the spirits to listen to your requests.

There are many more behaviors we could discuss in specificity, but instead, I will leave you with the overall advice of being more thoughtful in all areas of your life. Pay attention to the behaviors you engage in, and analyze the messages you might be unintentionally sending to your helping spirits. The way you care for your body, the way you eat, and how you interact with those around you are all part of your ceremonial work. The more energy you spend on something, the more you indicate to your helping spirits that this is what you hope to attract.

We must also learn to center our practices within the context of our lives. This does not refer only to our spiritual and emotional lives, but also the literal environment we work and live in. While teaching a workshop in Brooklyn, New York, I was explaining to the group of students that we start our journeys by envisioning ourselves in a meaningful place in nature. A couple of folks raised their hands, concerned they would not be able to journey, because the landscape they were familiar with was extremely urban. One woman asked if the size of her spot in nature mattered, because her special place was very small, as tends to happen in dense urban areas. Environmental issues aside (for now), the size of a natural space is not an impediment to a shamanic journey or practice. Every place in our world needs healing, and arguably urban centers need it most of all. Despite the lack of green space, urban centers still have helping spirits, many of whom are working hard to heal the land from the loss of the landscape and creatures that used to be there. The spirits of a place also take on the load of helping those who inhabit it, so the denser the urban center, the heavier the load these helping spirits have to bear. If you live in one of these places, I urge you to work on understanding what it means to do shamanic work within that context, and to extend your practice to the land and space around you, which we will discuss in greater depth later in this book.

As we start to reframe the way we look at and move through the world, we must continue to work on ourselves. Once of the most important lessons in living intentionally is learning to manage our ego. As we each work on tempering our ego, we also have to tackle the concept of power. One of the goals of shamanic practice is to increase our personal power. However—and this is a very important aside—the goal of power within Shamanism is not to have power over others. When we speak of power, we speak of personal sovereignty. The term *sovereignty* usually refers to a political state's ability to govern itself. Within the context of spiritual work, it refers to our power over ourselves. One of my teachers would always start ceremony by stating, "I am sovereign in this space. We are sovereign in this space." Through Shamanism, we learn how to take control of our bodies, minds, and lives, and how to wear our metaphorical crowns. When we evaluate our growth, the benchmarks lie completely within ourselves. We should not be comparing ourselves to others, or trying to gain power over others.

As shamanic practitioners we must also learn the lesson of personal responsibility. As we start to understand that we co-create our realities, there must be an accompanying understanding of responsibility. This means being discerning and intentional in our actions, and a willingness to face consequences. We also cannot continue to blame others for our experiences. We will never be able to control the behaviors of others, and it is inevitable that we will suffer trauma at the hands of others. However, we are responsible for how we react to these events and how we let them impact our paths. This does not mean we should deny our feelings in these circumstances. There is power in our emotions, and trauma is one of our most powerful teachers, which we will discuss later in this book. That said, we must learn how to process and integrate trauma in productive ways. We can always turn to our helping spirits in these moments.

There is one last concept that is absolutely crucial to shamanic practice: gratitude. We must come to understand that everything the earth provides us is a gift, and to express our gratitude for it.

Our shamanic work should never be approached with an attitude of entitlement. We should never believe that we are owed anything by the earth, by nature, or by our helping spirits. Everything they provide us is something to be profoundly thankful for; and the more we understand this, the more we can start seeing the abundance in our lives. As you develop your shamanic practice and engage with your helping spirits, always thank them for the medicine they are sharing with you.

Ultimately, the most important element of your shamanic practice is what you bring to it. Whatever form of ceremony you choose, you must come to it with the determination to allow change within yourself. The point of all the ritual work we do is to uncover our own depths and transform. Without this willingness, there is little purpose to engaging with our own psychological and emotional baggage.

EXERCISE

PRACTICING GRATITUDE

We have discussed the importance of gratitude, and this is truly a cornerstone of integrating Shamanism into your daily life. This is a quick and simple exercise that you can practice on a regular basis to engage in intentional gratitude. It will help you shift your perceptions and recognize the gifts that are offered to you on a daily basis.

Find a quiet place where you can be undisturbed for 10 to 15 minutes. Sit in a way that you can be comfortable and relaxed. Take several deep, slow breaths to clear your mind.

Speaking out loud, go through a list of gratitude. This is done out loud because our voices are powerful ceremonial tools. Below is an example of what these statements can look like, but you should thank our planet and nature for everything they have to offer.

❊ I am thankful for this planet.

❊ I am thankful for earth, air, fire, and water.

❋ I am thankful for the sun and how it sustains us.

❋ I am thankful for all of earth's creatures.

❋ I am thankful for my helping spirits and their guidance.

As you work through this exercise, get specific with your gratitude. Mention the specific things in your life you are thankful for, such as your home, your surroundings, your resources, anything that supports your life and brings you joy. Name the people who love you and support you. Thank the universe for providing the space and time to engage in this exercise, then take a few deep cleansing breaths before resuming your day.

❖ 6 ❖

ACHIEVING AN ALPHA STATE

ENTERING AN ALTERED STATE OF CONSCIOUSNESS is key to many spiritual and wellness practices, including but definitely not limited to Shamanism. Alpha states are the doorway to shamanic journeying. When we enter this state, we are more open and receptive to energies outside of ourselves. But what exactly does this mean? Our brain activity is measured in waves, and the frequency of these waves changes based on how alert or awake we are at any given moment. If you are more alert, your brain waves emit at a higher frequency. The less alert you are, the slower your brain waves, with the slowest being when you are in your deepest sleep. The more you can lower your brain waves while remaining awake, the deeper the trance state you can access.

The unit of measure for brain waves is hertz, which is a measure of cycles per second. When we are fully awake and alert, we are in a beta state, with brain waves measuring approximately 15 to 40 Hz. In an alpha state, we are awake but more relaxed and receptive. This happens at approximately 9 to 14 Hz. When our brain waves drop below 8 Hz, we enter a theta state, which usually indicates a deep trance, but can happen during daydreaming. When we are in a deep sleep, we enter a delta state, with brain waves generally measuring between 1.5 and 4 Hz.

There are many ways to enter an alpha state, including mental exercises, breathing techniques, meditation, and more. One popular technique for achieving an alpha state is square or box breathing, a technique that has been adopted so widely, it is used by Navy SEALs for stress reduction. This method is based on very intentional and rhythmic breathing. In Shamanism, the primary method for inducing an alpha state is through sonic driving. In a nutshell, sonic driving is the use of repetitive, rhythmic percussion, usually performed with a drum or a rattle.

The drumming performed for shamanic journeying includes different drumbeats that mark different moments in the journey. We start off the journey with four rapid drumrolls. In my training, these are four rapid drumrolls of four beats each, signaling a greeting to the four cardinal directions. I have also seen a variation of the opening, with four drumrolls of seven beats.

After the opening drumbeats, we move into the main drumming, which runs for about 15 to 30 minutes. This drumming should be rapid and repetitive. In his teachings, Michael Harner recommends a drumbeat of approximately 205 to 220 beats per minute. Jim PathFinder Ewing suggests approximately 180 beats per minute. I have experimented with slower and faster beats and prefer to focus on a beat that "feels" right rather than counting beats. If you find the drumbeat is pulling you out of a beta state and into a trance, then it is effective. As you listen to different recordings, or live drumming if you have the opportunity, or even start experimenting with drumming yourself, you will discover your own preference.

Once the 15 to 30 minutes are up, the drummer signals to the journeyer that is it time to return to ordinary reality. This is referred to as the callback. The drummer stops the repetitive drumming, performs the same set of four drumrolls from the opening sequence, and immediately goes into very rapid repetitive drumming for about 30 to 60 seconds. This should be fast, indicating that journeyers should retrace their steps back to Middle World. The journey then ends with a final set of four drumrolls.

To many indigenous cultures, the drumbeat reflects the pulse of Mother Earth. Drumming has been a part of human rituals for millennia and has the ability to reconnect us to our roots. It is part of our ancestral knowledge, which has been passed down in our DNA.

ORDINARY AND NON-ORDINARY REALITY: WHAT IS JOURNEYING?

SHAMANISM IS INHERENTLY ANIMISTIC. THIS means it is based on the belief that everything in nature—all creatures, plants, and landscapes—have a life force or vital essence. Closely tied to this is also the belief in two realities, commonly referred to as ordinary reality and non-ordinary reality. Ordinary reality is the reality most of us experience in our daily lives. It is the incarnate world, that which we see with our physical eyes and experience with our physical bodies. Non-ordinary reality is the spirit realm. This is where we are able to connect with the non-incarnate and the ethereal. We can communicate directly with the spirits of everything around us, and develop relationships with non-corporeal entities that are willing to help and guide us along our incarnate paths. These entities are our helping spirits, who we can collaborate with to co-create our realities.

The concept of co-creation is seen across many metaphysical and spiritual philosophies. Hermeticism is a metaphysical philosophy that focuses heavily on the nature of reality and universal principles of creation. The Hermetic tradition is based on the work of Hermes Trismegistus, which has greatly influenced many esoteric traditions. There are seven Hermetic Principles that explain how the universe works and how we can use this information to affect the world around us. The first Hermetic Principle is the Principle of Mentalism, which states that "All is Mind." This speaks both to the power of our minds and also to the nature of reality. Most Westerners tend to have a very limited view of reality, emphasizing the importance of physical touch and physical sight. Through journeying, we learn how to connect with reality that exists beyond the basic senses.

In Shamanism, we use sonic driving to trigger an alpha state so we can enter non-ordinary reality. This is what we refer to as journeying. In the most basic terms, journeying is a process through which we use visualization to travel to Lower or Upper Worlds and connect with our helping spirits to obtain guidance and healing. When we are in non-ordinary reality, we often perceive information in the form of symbols, archetypes, and metaphors. This is consistent with Carl Jung's theories regarding the human psyche and the collective unconscious.

The psyche consists essentially of images. It is a series of images in the truest sense, not an accidental juxtaposition or sequence, but a structure that is throughout full of meaning and purpose; it is a "picturing" of vital activities. And just as the material of the body that is ready for life has need of the psyche in order to be capable of life, so the psyche presupposes the living body in order that its images may live. (C. G. Jung, *Psychological Reflections: An Anthology of Jung's Writings 1905–1961* [London and New York: Routledge, 1998], p. 5)

Archetypes play a central role not only in Jungian psychology, but in many esoteric and spiritual traditions. For example, archetypes are a key element in tarot systems, especially within the symbolism depicted in the Major Arcana cards. We also come into contact with archetypes in Shamanic Journeying, as it is a way for our helping spirits to communicate with us using universal or near-universal symbolism.

A question that often comes up when students are learning to journey is: "Is what I'm seeing real, or am I imagining it?" I ask of my students that they try not to focus on this question. For those of us who work in both ordinary and non-ordinary reality, everything is real. When we see something with our mind's eye, rather than our physical eyes, this does not make it less real. Jung also wrote about thoughts and ideas, pointing out that even if we try to minimize them as imagination or delusion, this does not make them any less real or effective. Human imagination is a gift, and one that holds immeasurable power. When we journey, we engage in a process called *active imagination*. This term comes from Jungian psychology and refers to a process used to bridge the conscious and unconscious mind, so we can open up to the messages the universe has for us.

There is no difference in principle between organic and psychic formations. As a plant produces its flowers, so the psyche creates its symbols. (C. G. Jung, *Psychological Reflections: An Anthology of Jung's Writings 1905–1961* [London and New York: Routledge, 1998], p. 5)

Andrew Steed, a Celtic shaman and teacher, advises us to have experiences without putting parameters on ourselves. There is no incorrect shamanic journey experience, and only by entering the journey space with complete openness, without preconceptions or expectations, can we experience the most profound shifts.

The shamanic journey experience is unique to every person. The most common form of experiencing journeys is through visual imagery, where we "see" the journey play out in our mind's eye. However, this is not the only method for receiving information. We have five senses, and any of them can be activated during a journey, sometimes with more than one sense being activated during a single journey. If you are someone who struggles to see things in your mind, you may experience your journey through sound or touch. Some people never see or feel anything, but they receive information intuitively. Any and all of these forms of journeying are valid and powerful.

> The archetype—let us never forget this—is a psychic organ present in all of us. (C. G. Jung, *Psychological Reflections: An Anthology of Jung's Writings 1905–1961* [London and New York: Routledge, 1998], p. 46)

❖ 8 ❖

CEREMONIAL TOOLS AND POWER OBJECTS

WE CAN HAVE COUNTLESS CEREMONIAL tools and power objects for ritual use, but there are two specific tools that play an essential role in shamanic ceremony: the drum and the rattle. These instruments are ancient and resonate with us on a primal level. When we use drums and rattles, we are using tools and tapping into ritual practices that have been part of our genetic coding and ancestral memory for millennia. Research has shown that humans have genetic memory, which means that the ritual use of percussion is now part of our DNA. Genetic memory is knowledge passed down to us from our ancestors. In psychology, Carl Jung explores this within his concepts of archetype. Jung explains that humans are born with certain inherited, preprogrammed information that taps into the collective unconscious. This means we have access to knowledge we have not yet learned firsthand. We are genetically programmed to have a response to the use of these tools and the sound of percussion.

Rattles and drums have been part of human rituals for millennia, with archeological evidence showing their use as far back as early Mesopotamia and Ancient Egypt, and perhaps even farther. Catal Huyuk, estimated to have existed between 7500 to 5700 BCE, was a large Anatolian city located in present-day Turkey. Inhabitants' religious practices were goddess-oriented and made regular use of ritual drumming. Various statues and carvings of the goddess Cybele have been uncovered, featuring handheld drums.

The most commonly used style of drum in modern Shamanism is the handheld frame drum. You can use drumming as part of your soul song, to greet your helping spirits and shift the energetic vibration of the space you are working, and for shamanic journeying. It can be difficult to drum for yourself while simultaneously journeying, so I recommend finding audio of live drumming to use when journeying without someone to drum for you. Live drumming is always best, but a good audio file and noise canceling headphones will do the trick.

Rattles are also used to shift energetic vibrations, to greet helping spirits, and to honor the directions. Some cultures use rattles instead of drums for their journeys. In my personal practice, I use either my drum or my rattles, along with my voice, to honor the four cardinal directions before starting a ceremony. This helps set the intent in my mind to step out of mundane life and perform sacred work and also alerts and calls my helping spirits to participate.

When I refer to shifting energetic vibrations, I mean this in a rather literal sense. The noise produced by drums and rattles produces sound waves, as does any sound. When these sound waves are produced, they affect the energetic field of the space you are working in. They can also affect the energetic fields of objects, plants, animals, and people. If you are feeling stagnant energy, use your rattle to break up the energy around your body. You can do this yourself, or it can be performed by another practitioner who you feel comfortable with. Rattle close to your body, moving from your head down to your feet and moving over every part of your body. If a specific part of your body feels particularly stuck, give it extra attention.

As you embark on your shamanic practice, you will discover other power objects. Your helping spirits may ask you to honor them with specific symbols or talismans, which can become part of your altar. You may also develop relationships with plant and crystal allies. At the core of most shamanic systems is a belief that everything has an energetic vibration, and therefore, if used appropriately, can be used to affect change.

9

THE WOUNDED HEALER ARCHETYPE AND SOUL SONGS

OUR BODIES AND OUR SELVES ARE THE PRIMARY and most important ceremonial tools at our disposal. As such, we must learn to honor ourselves and better integrate our bodies, the material self, and our souls, the immaterial self. Learning to be in harmony with and within ourselves is one of the key processes of shamanic healing.

When people are called to Shamanism, they are generally seeking to heal profound wounds. They come to Shamanism to resolve aspects of their lives that are not in harmony. As we move through life, we experience trauma of varying degrees. Trauma chips away at our souls. It is common for people to come to Shamanism after experiencing particularly profound trauma, the kind that disrupts our foundation. The resulting wound becomes a catalyst for change, functioning as an initiation rite of sorts. This is the underlying concept of the Wounded Healer archetype: we grow and learn through suffering.

The archetype of the wounded healer is a recurring concept in many shamanic traditions, as well as other spiritual paths. Even though Jung coined the term, this concept can be seen in mythology throughout the world. Stories of wounded healers date as far back as Ancient Greece, seen in the myth of the centaur Chiron, as well as the legend of Asclepius. This archetype describes a being who has gone through a journey of self-transformation triggered by trauma. Within this concept is the understanding that from the wound comes a gift in the form of growth. More specifically, this gift generally manifests as a call for the wounded healer to help others heal their own wounds. The trauma results in a significant personal shift that allows us to gain wisdom that can be used in service of others.

Trauma is something that is overcome through a dynamic, multistage process. The wound urges us to transform, which in turn shifts the wound, encouraging another shift within ourselves. To face and accept a wound and embrace its teachings, as opposed to resorting to avoidance, is a key internal process for the shamanic practitioner. The trauma may awaken something new inside us, calling us to a new path, such as Shamanism. Through shamanic practice, we are able to start mending not only the original trauma, but our other traumas.

Suffering is such a transformative experience that some cultures, both shamanic and non-shamanic, will engage in intentional suffering within ceremonial context as a way to trigger internal shifts.

While I cannot disclose specific details, I have in my own initiatory rites experienced extended isolation, sleep deprivation, binding, and other forms of voluntary suffering. These experiences are powerful and transforming, but should not be entered lightly. In his book *Cave and Cosmos,* Michael Harner discusses the use of intentional suffering as a way to gain personal power from the helping spirits, describing examples of such rites among the Inuit, the Shuar, the indigenous tribes of the North American Great Plains, and tribes in the Upper Amazon region. This information is not provided to encourage readers who are new to this path to subject themselves to suffering (quite the contrary, as this should not be attempted without extensive prior experience), but rather to highlight the transformative potential of trauma. Every traumatic event we experience holds the power to push us forward on our spiritual paths.

As we discussed earlier in this book, the most important part of ceremony is approaching it with the true belief that we need to transform. In Shamanism, we engage in various forms of ceremony, such as power animal retrievals and soul retrievals, as part of our healing journeys. One such ceremony, which is perhaps the simplest but most important, is singing our soul songs. We discussed earlier the importance of our voices as ceremonial tools, and singing our soul songs is one important way we can use them.

One of my teachers once said there are two very important questions we must ask ourselves: When did we stop singing? And when did we stop dancing? Singing and dancing are the most primal expressions of self we can engage in as incarnate humans. Modern society tends to cast judgment on unrestrained singing and dancing, and the more time we spend repressing our natural voices and movements, the more we disconnect from crucial parts of our soul. Humans are the only beings in nature who apologize for their own voices. The wind does not apologize for howling, crickets do not apologize for chirping, and we should not apologize for making our most primal sounds. To do so is to deny an essential part of ourselves.

When should soul songs be used? They can be a practice of their own that we can engage in regularly to strengthen ourselves, or in conjunction with other shamanic work. I strongly recommend singing your soul song at the opening of any ceremonial work you engage in. By starting with your soul song, you are establishing a strong connection with your soul, creating a vibrational shift in the space you are working in, and indicating to your helping spirits that you are ready to participate in ceremony.

Your soul song is your most honest, unfiltered, and unplanned vocal expression. It is what happens when you close your eyes, move your lips, and let whatever sounds your soul wants to make in that particular moment come out. It is usually a song without words, a song that is brand new, and likely to be different every time, because it expresses whatever your soul needs in that very instance. You can drum or rattle as you sing, as this is another way for your body to express itself. The key element is for your soul song to be honest and free of fear or judgment.

The soul song is not limited to vocalization. Rather, I prefer to think of the soul song as the full, honest expression of the soul as manifested through the entire body. When singing our soul songs, we often feel called to dance as well. Surrender to this call and allow your body to move freely in honest expression. Engaging in song and dance is one of the most primal ways to honor ourselves and Spirit.

Soul songs can be sung both in solo ceremonies and in group settings. When singing soul songs in a group setting, each person sings their own particular soul song at the same time. Do not worry about whether your soul songs sound "good" together or whether they sound similar or different. Allow yourself to be vulnerable in the moment as you share in a vibrational shift in preparation for the work to follow. By engaging in soul songs as a group, all participants will be more in sync with each other and more open as they move into the next step of the shamanic work they are about to engage in.

EXERCISE

SINGING YOUR SOUL SONG

If you are feeling unsure or self-conscious, use this as a basic guideline to allow your soul song to come forward. You will need a drum or rattle and a quiet place. If you do not own any ceremonial tools, you can get creative. Fill a small jar with dry rice, dry beans, or even pebbles to use as a rattle.

Find a quiet space where you can be undisturbed for 15 to 20 minutes. This can be indoors or outdoors, as long as it is a place where you feel safe and comfortable.

Start rattling or drumming softly. Allow the sound to fill your body and mind, and start to move your body slowly. These do not have to be big movements. Start swaying slowly and let the movements grow instinctively. You can start rattling or drumming louder and faster if you feel called to.

Now begin vocalizing. Start with a soft hum and let it build. Open your mouth and let this hum become a song. Try not to worry about what it sounds like, but let it be genuine. It might be a single, monotone cry. It might turn into a melody, or be a repetitive single syllable. Let these sounds keep coming forward without words. As you continue to drum or rattle, start to dance, and sing, letting your inhibitions melt away. Increase the tempo if that feels right.

This is your soul song. It will probably sound different every time, because it always represents what you need to express in that particular moment.

You will know when to end your soul song because you will feel a change in your energy. When I sing my soul song, I will feel a light buzz in my head, which lets me know that my consciousness has started to shift. I end with a last, loud cry and rapid drumming or rattling.

10

JOURNEYING TO LOWER WORLD: CONNECTING WITH POWER ANIMALS

IN SHAMANISM, WE HAVE A COMMON BELIEF THAT everyone has at least one power animal that accompanies them throughout their life. In some cultures, this belief states that no person can survive beyond infancy without a power animal. As we move through life, other power animals will join us as we navigate particular challenges, and then they will move on. Even if we are not aware of them, they are still present and offering their medicine. But if we are able to find them and cultivate a relationship, we can reap great benefits. A central part of shamanic practice is to establish a working relationship with our power animals so that we can be intentional in our communications with them and make the most of the guidance they have to offer us. Power animals are animal-form spirit guides that embody the archetypal energies of a particular animal and that come forward to guide and support us as we move through our human lives.

The primary way to connect with our power animals is by journeying to Lower World. On these journeys, you may encounter many animal spirits, but not all will be your power animals. Your power animals are specific animal spirits who have offered themselves to be your helping spirits. They have specific medicine and healing to offer you on your life path.

Before going on your first journey, do your best to clear yourself of any preconceptions. This applies to both the experience of Lower World and your power animal. I often see newer practitioners arriving with the expectation of connecting with animals perceived as more powerful, such as Bear, Eagle, and Lion. It is extremely important to remember that all animal spirits have medicine and guidance to share. Whoever shows up for you is giving you the medicine you need right now. The medicines of Dragonfly and Bee are just as valuable and important as the medicine of Shark. Remember that in nonordinary reality, communication happens through symbolism and metaphor, and you are completely safe and in control. Your power animals may act in ways that seem threatening or perform actions that would be unpleasant in ordinary reality, but in Lower World, these actions are metaphors for the medicine they are offering you. Be open to whatever experiences you are offered. If you are ready to try your first journey, use the outline provided here to guide you.

To journey to Lower World, you will need the following:

❖ A quiet place where you can be uninterrupted for approximately 30 minutes

❖ A comfortable place to lie down that is not your bed, such as a yoga mat or a comforter you can place on the floor. I recommend not journeying in bed, as you are more likely to fall asleep.

❖ A light blanket, if you tend to get cold

❖ Comfortable clothing. You don't want to be distracted by physical discomfort.

❖ An eye cover, if your space can't be darkened

❖ A pillow to support your head (optional)

❖ Your audio recording of live drumming. I recommend a 15-minute drumming audio to start.

❖ A journal to chronicle your journey when you return

Before starting, take a moment to prepare your space. Using your drum or rattles, greet the four cardinal directions and invite your helping spirits to join you. Once you establish a relationship with the plant spirits, you may choose to burn certain herbs at this point. Anything you can do to signal to spirit that you are about to start ceremony helps establish a deeper connection. Once your space is prepared, sing your soul song to help open yourself up to the upcoming journey experience.

When you feel ready, lie down and make sure you are comfortable. You may need a pillow to support your head. Hold your clear intention in your mind. If this is your first time journeying, your intention should be to journey to Lower World and meet one of your power animals. If someone is drumming for you, signal to them that you are ready to begin, or start playing your drum recording.

Start the journey by visualizing yourself outdoors in a place in nature that is both familiar and comforting to you. This should be a real place you have visited, as it will be your tether to Middle World. Look for your entry into Lower World, which will be a path that can take you into the earth. It might be an opening in a tree, where you can enter and travel down the roots. It could be a cave leading downward, a deep body of water, or even a simple hole in the ground. Go into the opening and move through the earth, feeling the dirt, the dampness, and the rocks. As you keep moving, find the threshold that will take you into Lower World. It can be a door, a portal, or even an opening at the end of a tunnel. When you step through, you will find yourself in a new landscape. If you are experiencing visual stimuli, note what it looks like. If you do not see anything, remember that you have several other senses. Do you feel anything on your skin? Is the sun shining, or the wind blowing? Do you hear or feel anything? Reach out and feel the ground beneath your feet.

After taking a moment to orient yourself, you are ready to explore Lower World. Move through your landscape and see what you discover. Test the boundaries of the laws of physics and search for your power animal. In some shamanic traditions, there is the belief that if an animal shows itself to you at least three times, it is signaling to you that it is your power animal. In my personal practice, I have learned to directly ask any creature I encounter if it is one of my power animals. If it says no, it might simply move on, or it might help me along the path to find my animal. When you do find your power animal, thank it for showing itself and ask what it wants to share with you. Spend time with it and let it show you around.

If you find yourself waiting for something to happen, do not hesitate to give yourself a push. As discussed in the section on non-ordinary reality, to journey is to engage in a process called Active Imagination. Your journey is co-created with your helping spirits, but is not created entirely by them. When folks are struggling with their first journeys in my group circles, I encourage them to "see" the ground beneath their feet, to reach down and touch it, and to take a few steps. Your journey will begin to unfold, and you will find yourself in a place beyond your personal imagination.

When you hear the drumming calling you back, which will be signaled by a drumroll and then faster drumming, thank your power animal and retrace your steps. Find your way back to your entry point, and return to your starting point in Middle World. As the callback is wrapping up, you should be back where you started. Take a moment to recenter and reground in your body. When you feel ready, use your journal to write down your journey. You will want to revisit these notes later, when the details start to fade from your memory.

Do not be discouraged if you were not able to reach Lower World on your first journey. Journeying takes practice, especially for those of us who are not used to "seeing" with our mind's eye. I have met many shamanic practitioners who struggled in the beginning. If this happens to you, be patient with yourself and try again a few days later. It can sometimes take months to develop your journeying abilities. Also, sometimes we will reach Lower World but not encounter a power animal. Do not be discouraged by this either. Our power animals reveal themselves when we are ready, and sometimes they want us to focus on getting used to non-ordinary reality before introducing themselves.

Remember that every journey experience is valid and real, and we all experience non-ordinary reality in different ways. Many people go into their first journeys expecting vivid imagery as if they were watching a movie screen. This is rarely the case. Some people will have vivid visual journeys, while others may see very little but receive a lot of information intuitively. If you are someone who does not receive visual information, check in with your other senses. You might also find your visualization abilities grow over time as you practice. Jenn, a woman in my group, did not "see" anything in her first journey, but she received information through her other senses. Jenn felt cold all over her body except for her knees, which were radiating heat. Shortly after that, she was diagnosed by her doctor with cartilage loss in her knees. Information comes in many forms; we just have to be open to receiving it.

If you are journeying in a group, I recommend taking time for sharing and integration. Some practitioners believe that journeys should never be shared. Others believe that community is an integral part of the practice, and that we only gain a full understanding of our journeys when we share and open ourselves up to insight from others. I fall into the latter category, but with a caveat. Journeys are not to be shared with anyone and everyone. We share them in groups we trust, within sacred and safe space. What gets shared in the group setting does not leave the group. Whether you are sharing with a group or journeying by yourself, take a moment to wrap up your ceremony by thanking the helping spirits. If you do choose to share your experience with a group, make an effort to do so with an open mind. There are common themes that can pop up in journeys from person to person, but generally everyone's journey experience is unique. Some will experience journeys as having lasted days, and for others it will have felt like the blink of an eye. Every journey experience is valid and brings medicine, so try not to compare your experience to that of others.

After each journey, it is your responsibility to integrate the medicine of your power animals into your life. Our power animals help us as much as they can, but at the end of the day, we are responsible for ourselves. If your power animal gives you specific advice or asks you to perform a specific action, be sure to act on it. After all, if we do not act on the medicine they give us, we cannot enjoy its benefits. Many folks new to this practice ask me what their power animals symbolize. Some indigenous communities do have specific meanings they associate with different animals, but these meanings were developed over years of communicating with their guides. While there have been other books written on this topic, I recommend developing your own understanding of what and who your power animals are to you. If you ask your guides what their medicine is, they will tell you, and I would not be surprised if it differed from what you might find in a guidebook.

While there are a few common experiences that people report during power animal journeys, I recommend not reading this portion until after your first encounter with your power animal. This will allow you to have an unbiased experience rather than approaching it with expectations. After your first journey, you can review this section and see if you encountered any of these experiences.

Earlier in this book, we did briefly discuss the "feel" of Lower World. But what about the interactions we have with our power animals? Our helping spirits communicate in metaphors that often would not make sense in ordinary reality. One common way our power animals interact with us is through embodiment. This happens when we merge with our power animal while in a journey state. This is also called shape-shifting. There are dozens of different ways the merging can happen, such as entering the body of the power animal, or watching your body transform. If we experience this during a journey, understand that it is an extremely powerful way to connect with the power animal's medicine.

Another experience, which can be a bit jarring, is for our power animal to remove parts of our body. They may cut off a limb, or even reach into your body and remove a specific organ such as your heart or your kidney. This experience is called *dismemberment*. In some cases, our animals will take apart our entire bodies, in a process called *total dismemberment*. While such an experience in ordinary reality would be violent and painful, we must remember that non-ordinary reality functions differently. If your animal removes a piece of your body, it is pointing out an area that needs healing. It is removing an area where your energy is stuck. In the case of total dismemberment, your power animal is offering you very profound healing. If this happens to you, understand that your power animal is disassembling you so that you can dispel negative energies or break unhealthy cycles. This is the opportunity to put yourself back together in a healthier way.

If you did not experience embodiment or dismemberment, this absolutely does not mean that your journey was not valid, mean-ingful, or powerful. Whatever message your power animal had for you is what you need to know in that moment. Always keep in mind that many of the things you witness will be metaphorical rather than literal. If you see animals fighting, for example, they may be showing off their prowess, or enacting a conflict you are experiencing in your own life. As you become more experienced in journeying, you will become better acquainted with the language of your power animals.

11

HONORING YOUR POWER ANIMALS

WHEN MY STUDENTS ENCOUNTER THEIR POWER animals for the first time, some are surprised to find them to be quite impatient! Our power animals have been with us all along, often unacknowledged for years, and some are very eager to get to work once we finally establish contact with them. One of my students actually had her power animal exclaim "Finally!" on her first journey. Once you have taken this first step, it is very important to keep honoring and acknowledging them. If we develop a regular practice of communicating, honoring, and thanking them, we can enrich our lives with their guidance and blessings. On the other hand, think of instances in your life when you might have felt less than generous toward someone who did not appreciate your efforts. The most important way to honor your power animals is by taking their wisdom and guidance to heart and implementing it in your life. But beyond that, they do like to be thanked and honored in other ways, too. That said, you are not obligated to follow every piece of advice your power animals give you. There is room for respectful disagreement in these relationships. There are also other ways to thank and honor your power animals.

A great way to honor your power animal is through song and dance. This can be as simple as moving your body as your animal would, which is referred to as "dancing your power animal." Do they move slowly or quickly? Do they move in large, bounding leaps, or smaller, calculated steps? Try to embody their movements. Allow yourself to become completely immersed in the experience. Mimic their sounds and mannerisms. Sometimes our power animals will dance or perform for us during a journey. If they do, pay close attention, because they are providing you with a gift. You can mimic the dance they showed you as a way to strengthen your connection with them, honor them, and increase your personal power. Make a regular practice of singing and dancing for your power animal, as it will keep strengthening your relationship.

You can also honor them by setting up an altar in their honor in your home and filling it with special objects and images. There is no single way to set up an altar. Altars can be huge and elaborate, or small and minimalist. Your altar can be as simple as a representation of your animal, such as a picture or figurine, and a small offering. If you cannot have a visible altar in your home, it can take the form of a small box or a dresser drawer that you can fill with power objects. If you are creatively inclined, consider painting, drawing, or sculpting the image yourself. I do recommend having offerings on your altar, which can be a favorite food of your power animal, seasonal flowers, or anything that feels meaningful. If you are feeling unsure, next time you journey you can ask your power animal or animals how they would like to be honored. You may even find that their preferences change over the years.

We want the energies of our power animals to be present in our lives. The more we make space for them, the more their healing energy will permeate all aspects of our lives. In addition to setting up an altar for them, we can carry their images on our persons as we move through daily life. We might not be able to dance our power animals before walking into an important meeting at work (though if you have a private space to do so, try it!), but having a necklace or key chain with their image will help you connect with them and feel supported. If you do not wear jewelry, carrying a small figurine in your pocket works, too. Some of us also choose to honor our power animal through impermanent and permanent markings on our bodies. You can paint ritual markings on your body before ceremony to help you embody your power animal. There are some practitioners who choose to have a images of their power animals tattooed on their bodies. While this is not a decision to be made lightly, ritual tattooing is seen in many spiritual practices across the globe.

As you become more experienced, you will develop your own knowledge of the best way to honor your power animals. The suggestions I have provided here are by no means exhaustive, so I encourage you to get creative. As long as you approach this process with sincerity, your power animals will appreciate your efforts.

❖ 12 ❖

JOURNEYING TO UPPER WORLD: CONNECTING WITH ANCESTRAL HELPING SPIRITS

JUST AS WE ALL HAVE POWER ANIMALS, WE ALSO have human-form teachers looking to help and guide us. All spirit entities can travel to any of the spiritual dimensions, but our human-form guides are generally found in Upper World. Before we journey in search of our ancestral helping spirits, it is important that we understand that they are a very specific type of ancestral spirit. Not everyone leaves their earthly form to become a helping spirit. While every person crosses over to the spirit realm at the end of their incarnate lives, not every soul will become resolved after crossing over. Some souls carry unresolved karma and emotional baggage, making them inappropriate to act as helping spirits. If you consult with these ancestors, you may find their advice to be rooted in their own traumas and fears. Ancestral helping spirits are resolved spirits, meaning they reconnected with the source after passing, becoming whole again. These ancestral helping spirits have chosen to return and act as guides. When we journey, it is these resolved spirits we want to connect with. As we have addressed before, you should approach your journeys to Upper World without expectations or pre-conceptions. Ancestral helping spirits come in many forms and may surprise you. Sometimes we see family members, or famous teachers, or even children. Whoever shows up for you has the correct message to share with you in that moment.

Prepare for your journey to Upper World, in the same way you did for Lower World. You will need the following:

❋ A quiet place where you can be uninterrupted for approximately 30 minutes

❋ A comfortable place to lie down that is not your bed, such as a yoga mat or a comforter you can place on the floor. I recommend not journeying in bed, as you are more likely to fall asleep.

❋ A light blanket, if you tend to get cold

❋ Comfortable clothing. You don't want to be distracted by physical discomfort.

❋ An eye cover, if your space can't be darkened

❋ A pillow to support your head (optional)

❋ Your audio recording of live drumming. I recommend a 15-minute drumming audio to start.

❋ A journal to chronicle your journey when you return

When you are comfortable, close your eyes and start your drumbeat. Hold your intent clear in your mind, which is to journey to Upper World and meet one of your ancestral helping spirits. I find it helpful to ask one of my power animals to show up and help me find my way to Upper World.

Start your journey in Middle World by visualizing yourself in a space in nature that feels safe to you. I usually find that one of my power animals is waiting for me, as requested. From your starting point, look for an elevated place you can access, such as the top of a tall tree or a mountain. Some practitioners imagine elevators into the clouds, though I personally dislike using man-made machinery in my journeys. Experiment with different approaches, so you can find what works best for you. Make your way up, and once you reach the top of this place, allow yourself to continue moving upward into the sky, far above the earth. Keep traveling upward into the atmosphere until you encounter a membrane separating Middle World from Upper World. This membrane is a tangible boundary, and you can access Upper World only by crossing it. Without finding this transition point, you will keep traveling upward endlessly within Middle World. If you do not find it on your first try, do not be discouraged. Take a break and try again later. On my first attempt, I spent the entire time wandering around a cloud layer but did not manage to leave Middle World. I had been journeying to Lower World for years, but found the threshold to Upper World much more difficult to access. My second journey was far more successful.

Once you do encounter this membrane, move through it and arrive in Upper World. Take the time to notice your surroundings, making sure to check in with of all your senses. Are you seeing, smelling, feeling, or hearing anything? Move around Upper World and get to know your surroundings. You will probably find Upper World very different from Lower World. If you were accompanied by a power animal, you can request their help in finding your ancestral helping spirit. In my experience, our human-form guides can be a bit hesitant to fully reveal themselves on the first encounter. They may keep their faces shadowed or covered by a veil. Be willing to accept this, as they will probably reveal themselves once you are more familiar with one another. In the meantime, enjoy their company and ask them what information or guidance they have to offer you. Like our power animals, they have endless wisdom to share and it comes in many forms. In some of my journeys, my ancestral helping spirits have taught me very specific healing rituals, which I then incorporated into my ceremonial practices. They may teach you power ceremonies, songs, incantations, or many other powerful lessons.

When you hear the callback drumming, be sure to thank your ancestral helping spirits for their guidance before retracing your steps. Find your way back to your starting point, passing through the boundary membrane as you return to Middle World. As your journey wraps up, take the time to ease back into your body before moving. Record your experiences in your journal so you can revisit them later. We often need time to process the full meaning of the messages received from our guides, and it is very helpful to have an account of our journey to remind us of the details.

You have now received basic guides for how to journey both to Lower and Upper Worlds. These are practices you should engage in regularly so you can keep learning from your helping spirits. I have found that journeying at least once a month is a good schedule to keep feeling connected. If you are able to do so more often, I definitely encourage it.

✤ 13 ✤

HONORING THE ANCESTORS

HONORING OUR ANCESTORS IS AN IMPORTANT part of shamanic practice. As Shamanism aims to help us exist in harmony with ourselves, the planet, and the spirit realm, it also urges us to recognize our place within the story of humankind. We all have ancestors, and we will all have descendants, as our legacy continues whether or not we personally procreate. This happens in a variety of ways. When our bloodline continues through our family members, those future generations are also part of our legacy. But legacy extends beyond the physical transmission of DNA. Our legacies also continue when we share knowledge and experiences. Acknowledging this gives us a reminder that we are a small part of a much larger whole. It teaches us that in the same way the karma of our ancestors plays out in our lives, our karma will play out in the lives of our descendants. With this in mind, we should always make space in our personal practices to thank and honor all who came before us.

In the previous section, we discussed the difference between our ancestors and our ancestral helping spirits. Our ancestors are all of those who came before us, whereas our ancestral helping spirits are resolved beings who help us with our incarnate paths. While we only want to establish working relationships with the latter, both types of ancestors should be thanked and honored.

To honor your ancestral helping spirits, set up a shrine or altar just for them. If you want to set up an altar for your ancestors in general (unresolved or otherwise), make it a separate shrine from the one for your ancestral helping spirits. These altars generally do not have images of our deceased family members. Instead, they are filled with power objects and offerings for your helping spirits. They can be items such as bells, stones, and other objects that resonate with you. The offerings usually are seasonal flowers and plants, as well as foods left in special dishes. As you begin to develop a relationship with your ancestral helping spirits, you can and should request their help on specific projects in your life. They can help you overcome difficult situations and succeed at new endeavors. As your working relationship evolves, it will be important to thank them for their help through offerings, and you can journey to ask them how you can best honor them.

We have discussed how to meet our ancestral helping spirits and how to honor them, but this is just the beginning of the ancestral work that Shamanism opens us up to. This brings us to why we should honor even those ancestors who are still unresolved. It is important that we situate ourselves within our lineage, as it helps provide context for who we are and who we want to become. The more we understand our place in the bigger picture of our ancestral lines, the better we can define our goals. We all carry ancestral patterns of thought and behavior that are passed down through the generations. If we are to truly heal ourselves, we must address these inherited wounds. This type of work is referred to as *ancestral healing*.

Trauma affects us on a genetic level. Epigenetic research is uncovering that childhood trauma affects our DNA and can have an impact on our health later in life. Traumas our ancestors experienced have been passed down to us genetically, spiritually, and psychologically. Part of our duty to our descendants is to prevent trauma from continuing to be transferred to future generations. The only way to do this is by confronting this baggage we carry and working toward resolving it, so that we can end the cycles of perpetuation.

Asking your helping spirits for guidance is always a good place to start any healing work. Just remember that you want to journey either to your power animals or to your ancestral helping spirits, not to the unresolved ancestors themselves. Research has shown that severe trauma can become encoded in our DNA, so while part of your wounds are your own, some have been passed down to you. Shamanism provides you with tools that can help you heal trauma, both personal and inherited.

❖ 14 ❖

ENVIRONMENTAL SHAMANISM

For all of us, becoming indigenous to a place means living as if your children's future mattered, to take care of the land as if our lives, both material and spiritual, depended on it.

—ROBIN WALL KIMMERER, BRAIDING SWEETGRASS

AS SHAMANIC PRACTITIONERS, WE HAVE A responsibility to care for our land in the same way we care for ourselves. In the previous section, we discussed the importance of understanding our place within the story of human-kind. Just as we need to care for our descendants in our journeying practice, we have to care for the planet, so our descendants will also have a place to call home.

In her book *Braiding Sweetgrass: Indigenous Wisdom, Scientific Knowledge, and the Teachings of Plants*, Robin Wall Kimmerer asks us to shift the way we view the world. Our capitalist economy has turned the world into a resource to be mined, and all its gifts into commodities. If we can return to the ways of our ancestors and instead see the world as a gift, we can transform our relationship with it. If we understand everything as a gift, suddenly our lives are filled with abundance instead of scarcity. Kimmerer also discusses the gift economy, and the true meaning of a gift. There was a time when we understood that a gift was not a free thing, but rather the development of a relationship with responsibilities. The earth provides us with gifts, and it is our responsibility to care for her in return. For this reason, I see environmental Shamanism as an absolute necessity.

Our earth is hurting. It is undeniable that our planet is in a state of peril. Our goal as shamanic practitioners is to live in harmony with ourselves, the spirits, and with the earth. If you pursue a shamanic practice, I urge you to include healing for the planet as part of your regular practice. Our bodies are a reflection of the earth, in that we are the microcosm and the planet is the macrocosm. Earlier in this book, I mentioned the Hermetic Principles. The second principle is the Principle of Correspondence, which states that as above, so below; as within, so without. We have the capacity to create change in the world by healing ourselves; and by healing the world, we heal ourselves. It is our duty, as humans and shamanic practitioners, to actively contribute to the healing of the planet. Once you have enough practice and are ready to journey in Middle World, this is a practice I strongly encourage every shamanic practitioner to engage in regularly.

I once attended an immersive workshop at a remote retreat center in Rowe, Massachusetts, away from largely populated areas and outside of cell phone reception range. The center functioned solely as housing and gathering spaces for events centering on education and spiritual expansion. As a result, the spirits of this place were always hard at work, tending to a place that acted as a container for hundreds of people passing through and experiencing significant internal shifts. There was a significant energetic load to be managed by the helping spirits of the place. The teacher of the workshop tasked our group, during our last shamanic journey of the event, to journey to those helping spirits and ask them how we could honor them and contribute our energies to help sustain the retreat center.. We were asked by the spirits to perform a variety of honoring acts, from dancing to clapping to singing in order to give of ourselves to the place that had held us as we learned and grew.

This is a concept that can and should be employed in any and all places that need healing. Start on a smaller scale, with your own town or city for example. Since this journey will take place in Middle World, you will start by visualizing yourself in your home, and simply step out of your own front door. Keep moving and journey around your city and see what areas or neighborhoods are crying out for help. Ask your helping spirits to accompany you and show you what you can do to help. They will reveal specific tasks you can undertake. For example, I have charged quartz crystals with healing energy and then hidden them in places that needed it, such as the base of a tree growing in an ailing neighborhood. You may be asked to bring an offering of herbs, or perhaps to clap or rattle to dispel stagnant energy.

This exercise can be performed on any scale. Once you have journeyed around your city, broaden your reach. You can scan your whole state, the entire country, and even the whole planet. During one such journey, I found myself at the North Pole; it was crying out for help, asking for healing to help counter the damage done by the melting polar ice caps. When you reach a place that is asking for attention, find the helping spirits of the place and ask your own helping spirits to provide them with the help they need. The world has many problems beyond the scope and ability of any single person, but if each of us does our part, we will have a cumulative effect.

WHEN WE CALL A PLACE BY NAME IT IS TRANSFORMED FROM WILDERNESS TO HOMELAND.

—ROBIN WALL KIMMERER, *BRAIDING SWEETGRASS*

EXERCISE

PRACTICING ENVIRONMENTAL SHAMANISM IN YOUR NEIGHBORHOOD

This is an easy way to start developing a relationship with and offering healing to the neighborhood you live in. Crystals are great allies for shamanic work and can be used very effectively for environmental Shamanism. All crystals have their own energy or spirit, and we can work with them to shift the vibrations around us.

Gather a few small pieces of clear quartz crystal that you can leave as offerings. Clear quartz is great for channeling and amplifying energy. Sit for a few minutes and hold the quartz pieces in your hand. Ask your helping spirits to help you in setting the intention that these crystal pieces will be used to heal their surroundings. Hold that intent clear in your mind and focus on the crystals. If you feel called to, rattle or drum to increase the vibration as you focus your intent.

When you are ready, place them in your bag or pocket and go for a walk around your neighborhood. The intent of this walk is to find places that need a bit of energy help, and leave small crystals in these areas. Ask your helping spirits to accompany you on this walk and lend their energy as well.

As you walk through these familiar places, try to look at them with new eyes. If you have nature in your neighborhood, see if you notice ailing trees. You can bury a crystal near the tree to help it heal. If you know of places that stray animals or wildlife inhabit, find a place to leave a crystal to protect them. You can also leave crystals near intersections where accidents tend to happen or areas where homeless folks tend to gather. Our transient populations are very much in need of healing.

I once had a student who lived in a newer neighborhood built on land that used to be a forest. Once she discovered this, she realized she wanted to show her gratitude to the land and help heal it from the trauma of deforestation. She now regularly walks around her neighborhood looking for places to leave healing crystals.

At the end of your walk, restate your intent to bring healing to your neighborhood and thank your helping spirits for their support.

I recently had a conversation about Shamanism with a woman whom I was meeting for the first time. I told her of my personal goal to engage in more environmental Shamanism, especially as it pertains to Salem, Massachusetts, where I live. Salem has a dark history of violence and persecution, especially within the contexts of gender and religious freedom, and the land still bears these energetic scars. In recent decades, Salem has shifted to become a place where people gather to freely explore different spiritual paths, a powerful change from the era of the Witch Trials. The spirits who tend to Salem have had a heavy load on their shoulders. As a woman following a spiritual path very much outside what would have been acceptable during the Witch Trials, I consider it my personal responsibility to help and support our local spirits as Salem continues to heal and transform.

During our conversation, this woman and I spoke of the importance of connecting to the places we call home and assuming responsibility for their healing. As we got deeper into this discussion, she confided in me that she had been leaving offerings to the helping spirits of her own home for years. Her historic home was the site of horrible violence, and she had felt the calling to leave these offerings as a way to aid in healing the energetic wound of the place. As we talked about Shamanism, she came to realize she had been practicing environmental Shamanism all along.

As you start to work with the helping spirits of the land you call home, ask them to tell you the name of the land. This is part of developing a reciprocal relationship with the place you inhabit and acknowledging its importance. Many of us no longer live in the same places where we were born. Just as we must consider both our ancestors and our descendants in our shamanic work, so we must honor both the lands we came from and the lands we have chosen.

In my most recent trip back to my native land, I spent a lot of time in the ocean. Nothing feels as much like home to me as the oceans of my childhood. As I swam and danced in the breaking waves, humming a song of gratitude for the gift of that moment, I started to watch the trash rolling in the water. It made my heart hurt to see how much we have disrespected the earth. I made an offering to this place and its helping spirits, to gather as much trash as I could. At first, I was grabbing handfuls of wrappers. After I made the commitment to help, larger pieces of debris started flowing toward me as I stood in the water. Small wrappers gave way to trash bags, and, finally, a large, tattered duffel bag. I walked back and forth between the water and the land, dragging everything to a garbage bin, as the other beachgoers watched. None of us can clean the entire planet on our own, but if we each do our part, we will feel the collective effect. As I was leaving the beach that day, I saw a tlittle girl running to the edge of the water and back to her mother over and over. I realized she was picking trash out of the water, too. I walked up to her mother and told her how proud I was of her daughter.

> IF A MAN IS CAPABLE OF LEADING A RESPONSIBLE
> LIFE HIMSELF, THEN HE IS ALSO CONSCIOUS OF HIS
> DUTIES TO THE COMMUNITY.
>
> —CARL JUNG, *PSYCHOLOGICAL REFLECTIONS*

EXERCISE

MEETING THE SPIRITS OF A PLACE

Once you are comfortable journeying, this is a Middle World journey you can use to bring healing to a place, such as your neighborhood or even your whole city. It does not have to be a place where you live; it can be any place you are familiar with that is in need of healing.

Set aside at least 30 minutes of time and prepare for your journey. When you are ready, hold the intent in your mind to journey in Middle World to meet the spirits of the place you have chosen. Ask one of your power animals to meet you and guide you on this visit.

Once the drumming starts, see yourself in your home or another safe place in Middle World. This will be the starting point for your journey. You will not be traveling downward or upward this time, but instead moving around Middle World. If your power animal did not meet you there, ask it to join you and protect you.

With your power animal, travel to the place you want to heal. Whether it is your own neighborhood or a faraway place, once you arrive, you'll want to explore your surroundings. The goal is to find the helping spirit or spirits of the place. When you do find them, ask how you can contribute to their work. They will usually give you a specific task to perform after your journey. When you receive the information, thank them for their work and guidance and return to your starting point. Before returning to your body, thank your power animal for accompanying you.

You may find their request was rather odd, but know that it is the energy exchange they need from you. In one such journey, I was asked to clap for the trees. While I am sure I seemed a bit eccentric walking around clapping at plants, this was a way to give of my own energy to help heal the land. Clapping works in similar ways to a rattle, shifting the energetic vibrations in an area. Sometimes they will ask for offerings rather than actions. Whatever they ask of you, the important part is the willingness to be an agent for healing.

❖ 15 ❖

BEYOND THE BASICS

WITH THIS BOOK, I HAVE AIMED TO PROVIDE A framework for bringing Shamanism into your life. It gives you the basic information you need to go on your first journeys and establish contact with your helping spirits. As your practice develops, your journeys can encompass very specific goals. You can journey to your helping spirits to ask for guidance and advice in any area of your life, such as personal decisions, questions about career choices, and even guidance on relationships. You can also ask your helping spirits to provide you with powerful personal symbols to use in your daily life to bring you protection, inspiration, motivation, or any type of energy you are looking to attract. Just remember to always take the time to honor and thank them, and to occasionally journey just to visit and spend time with them. Our relationships with our helping spirits must be reciprocal, and we should always remember our responsibility to give back, just as we would with any interpersonal relationship in the incarnate plane.

The information provided here is just the beginning of where Shamanism can take you. Journeying is a crucial shamanic ceremonial practice, but it is far from the only one. If practitioners pursue the role of serving their communities, they will begin to take on other responsibilities, such as healing ceremonies, rites of passage, and end-of-life care. If you choose to pursue a path as a healer, remember that you must never perform work on others without their permission, even if you believe they would benefit from it. If you want to send healing to a person who is unable to consent, you can journey to their helping spirits and let them be the intermediary. I also strongly recommend developing a steady, regular practice and having established, active relationships with your helping spirits before engaging in this type of work. That said, here is an overview of some of these ceremonies, so you can begin to understand the depths that shamanic work can achieve.

One type of healing ceremony is soul retrieval, a powerful method for healing the deficits caused by what shamanic traditions refer to as *soul loss*. Soul retrievals are the shamanic approach to resolving soul loss and its associated symptoms. In Shamanism, we believe that people lose pieces of their soul when they experience trauma. This can be emotional or psychological trauma, such as heartbreak or abuse, or physical trauma, such as a serious injury or violence. Soul loss can even occur in moments of extreme fright, such as in a near-miss car accident. Many of us can probably remember being a passenger in a vehicle where the driver slammed on the brakes, narrowly avoiding an accident. When this happens we usually experience a harsh jolt, which produces a feeling that can be described as if we are leaving our bodies. Through a shamanic lens, this is actually what is happening. In that moment of shock, your soul momentarily leaves your physical body. When your soul snaps back, a fragment can be lost in the process.

Any experience of pain or trauma is a situation that may result in soul loss. While this might sound alarming, it is actually a very important coping mechanism. Soul loss allows us to become somewhat desensitized in order to withstand the experience. In cases of extreme trauma, this can be the only way someone manages to survive. In the field of psychology, this process is called *dissociation*. Dissociation can be described as a sense of detachment from one's life to varying degrees. People suffering from dissociation often describe feeling as if they are spectators rather than participants in their own lives. This is a result of soul loss. Once our soul pieces become lost they do not return on their own, and we continue to move through life slightly incomplete until this is resolved. Psychology addresses dissociation through psychotherapy. In Shamanism, we heal soul loss through the process of soul retrieval. These two approaches are not at odds, and in fact, there is great value in using them in tandem.

Through soul retrieval ceremonies, we can start to gather these soul pieces and bring them back to ourselves. Soul retrievals are usually performed by an experienced healer rather than something we do for ourselves. However, this is not an absolute rule. Once you have developed a regular journeying practice and have established a relationship with your helping spirits, you can perform soul retrievals for yourself. That said, the soul retrieval process is not one to be undertaken lightly. The retrieval itself is only the first step of the process. Once our soul pieces return, there is a necessary and important process of integration. There is generally an adjustment period after receiving a soul retrieval. We might be confronted with feelings we have been avoiding and possibly start experiencing a new depth of emotions. For this reason, I recommend having the support of an experienced healer for your first soul retrieval.

Earlier in this book, I discussed Shamanism as a system of direct revelation, where all participants perform their own journeys and communicate directly with their own helping spirits. As you progress along this path, you will be tapping into ancient wisdom, even if you do not realize it in the moment. The more you work with your helping spirits, the more you will understand the extent of the knowledge they can share with you.

I often have newcomers with no prior journey experience in drum circles I host. On one particular occasion, there was a woman who happened to come across the event online. She came on a whim, drawn in by curiosity. We started the ceremony by greeting the cardinal directions and singing our soul songs, and then I guided the group on a journey to Lower World. Afterward, we sat in circle and shared our stories as part of the integration process. When it was her turn, she shared that not only had she met her power animal, but that he told her she had lost a piece of her soul. He said he was taking care of it until she was ready to get it back. This is a great example of the power and effectiveness of journeying. This woman had no prior knowledge of Shamanism and yet she learned about soul loss directly from her helping spirits.

As I mentioned at the beginning of this chapter, shamans also serve their communities, sometimes through end-of-life care. This involves tending to those who are at the end of their earthly lives and helping them transition smoothly to the spirit realm. This type of shamanic work is referred to as *psychopomp*. This word is derived from Greek and means "guide of souls." The original meaning of psychopomp referred to mythological entities who helped newly deceased souls cross over to the other side. In the context of Shamanism, psychopomp refers to the ceremonial work of helping the dying cross over successfully. It also encompasses helping the souls that did not cross over completely after their bodies died. Not every soul crosses over successfully, remaining stuck in Middle World for a variety of reasons. They may have passed away with unresolved issues, died in a violent accident, or perhaps they do not even realize they are no longer alive. Through journeying, the shaman will track unresolved souls and help them complete their passage so they can reunite with the source.

Learning how to perform soul retrievals and psychopomp ceremonies is beyond the scope of this book, but it is a concept you can begin exploring if you hope to become a healer. In a previous chapter, we discussed the importance of managing our egos in shamanic work. This becomes especially important when acting as a healer for others. Healers act as instruments or vessels for messages from helping spirits in a process known as *becoming a hollow bone*. Whenever we are gathering information from the helping spirits, especially on the behalf of others, we should aim to act as a conduit apart from our own minds and egos. Furthermore, we must learn how to share these messages without viewing them through the lens of our own histories and emotional baggage. If we allow our own biases to impact how we deliver the messages of Spirit, we are interfering with the medicine that is trying to come through.

Becoming a hollow bone is an active and ongoing learning process. We all carry traumas and biases that impact both our actions and our perceptions. This is not inherently negative, but it is important to develop an understanding of where our biases lie. Here we can see another parallel to the field of psychology. Psychotherapists in training are usually encouraged to seek therapy for themselves, so they can identify their own baggage before providing therapy services to others. If you want to perform healing work, you must heal yourself first and foremost. As we explored in our discussion of the Wounded Healer archetype, our wounds can act as initiatory experiences. They force us to grow and expand. However, we must also have an understanding of how these wounds have shaped us, so that they do not interfere in our work of healing others.

Japanese Reiki, which we also discussed earlier in this book as a form of shamanic healing, is an example of becoming a hollow bone to perform healing ceremonies. When we provide energy healing without proper guidance, we are usually giving of our own ki and harming ourselves in the process. Through Reiki training, we learn how to become conduits for universal ki so we can channel it in an intentional manner to heal others. Rather than using our own ki, we become conduits for universal Ki, acting as the hollow bone. This is an important aspect of spiritual training, even if you do not go on to become a healer. By learning to set aside your ego, you will be better able to accept the lessons provided by your helping spirits.

Now that you have a comprehensive foundation for starting on your shamanic path, I encourage you to get as much firsthand experience as possible. Your best teachers are your helping spirits. I often meet students who spend months, if not years, reading books and studying but finding themselves afraid to put any of it into practice. You will learn much more through direct revelation than from any book or workshop. If you only take one lesson away from this book, let it be that there is no incorrect way to connect with the spirit realm. Shamanism is a collection of direct experiences, and the only way to develop your own practice is by having these experiences.

REFERENCES AND RESOURCES

Books

Between the Realms, Andrew Steed

The Way of the Shaman, Michael Harner

Cave and Cosmos: Shamanic Encounters with Another Reality, Michael Harner

When the Drummers Were Women: A Spiritual History of Rhythm, Layne Redmond

Reiki Shamanism: A Guide to Out-of-Body Healing, Jim PathFinder Ewing

Braiding Sweetgrass: Indigenous Wisdom, Scientific Knowledge, and the Teachings of Plants, Robin Wall Kimmerer

Psychological Reflections: An Anthology of Jung's Writings 1905–1961, Edited by Jolande Jacobi

The Cosmic Template: A Shamanic Month Minder for the Evolving Soul, Grace Walsh

The Kybalion, Three Initiates

The Norse Shaman: Ancient Spiritual Practices of the Northern Tradition, Evelyn Rysdyk

The Shaman's Toolkit: Ancient Tools for Shaping the Life and World You Want to Live In, Sandra Ingerman

Spirit Walking: A Course in Shamanic Power, Evelyn Rysdyk

Weather Shamanism: Harmonizing Our Connection with the Elements, Nan Moss and David Corbin

Online Resources

https://lastmaskcenter.org - Last Mask Center for Shamanic Healing

www.ana-campos.com - My personal website, with workshops and writings

http://thecrowmother.com - Energetic Healing. Tarot. Intuitive Counseling.

http://www.ayahuasca-ayllu.com/ - Centro de Sanación Ayahuasca Ayllu

http://www.shamanism.org - The Foundation for Shamanic Studies

http://spiritpassages.com/ - Trainings and Healing Sessions by Evelyn Rysdyk and Allie Knowlton

NOTES

INDEX

ABOUT THE AUTHOR

Ana Campos is a Shamanic Witch, Reiki Master Teacher, mixed-media artist, and artisan. She began her metaphysical training in her native country of Brazil and has a background in various lineages of witchcraft, shamanic methodologies, divination systems, and Reiki traditions. She hosts regular workshops and Shamanic Journey circles throughout New England. Ana lives in Salem, Massachusetts, and owns Circle of Stitches, a small shop focusing on fiber arts and metaphysical goods. Find out more at www.ana-campos.com.